What Do You Know About
Forces and
Motion?

PowerKiDS
press

Tilda Monroe

New York

Published in 2011 by The Rosen Publishing Group, Inc.
29 East 21st Street, New York, NY 10010

First Edition

Editor: Amelie von Zumbusch
Book Design: Kate Laczynski
Layout Design: Ashley Burrell
Photo Researcher: Jessica Gerweck

Photo Credits: Cover © www.iStockphoto.com/Joe McDaniel; p. 5 © www.iStockphoto.com/Jacek Chabraszewski; p. 6 (right) © www.iStockphoto.com/Rich Legg; pp. 6 (left), 7, 10, 11, 12, 14, 15, 17 (bottom), 18, 19, 20, 21, 22 www.Shutterstock.com; p. 8 © www.iStockphoto.com/Renee Lee; p. 9 © www.iStockphoto.com/Shawn Gearhart; p. 13 Jupiterimages/Getty Images; p. 16 Mike Kemp/Getty Images; p. 17 (top) © www.iStockphoto.com/Wojciech Gajda.

Library of Congress Cataloging-in-Publication Data

Monroe, Tilda.
 What do you know about forces and motion? / Tilda Monroe. — 1st ed.
     p. cm. — (20 questions. Physical science)
 Includes index.
 ISBN 978-1-4488-0673-7 (library binding) — ISBN 978-1-4488-1254-7 (pbk.) — ISBN 978-1-4488-1255-4 (6-pack)
 1. Force and energy—Juvenile literature. 2. Motion—Juvenile literature. I. Title.
 QC73.4.M64 2011
 531'.6—dc22
                                    2010000897

Manufactured in the United States of America

CPSIA Compliance Information: Batch #WS10PK: For Further Information contact Rosen Publishing, New York, New York at 1-800-237-9932

Contents

The Forces That Move the World 4

1. What is force? 6

2. Can we see force? 7

3. Does every object take the same amount of force to move? 8

4. Can several forces act on an object at the same time? 8

5. Does force always cause movement? 9

6. When I push something, does it always push me back? 10

7. Is that what happens when I let go of a balloon full of air? 11

8. What happens if I use force on a moving object? 12

9. Will an object move if no force acts on it? 12

10. Does this mean that a ball will keep rolling forever? 13

11. What kind of forces stop motion? 14

12. Why does a ball continue moving longer than a block? 15

13. What force makes two magnets move toward each other? 16

14. Why do magnets sometimes push away from each other? 16

15. Can you see magnetism in nature? 17

16. What force causes an apple to fall to the ground? 18

17. Why can't I kick a ball into outer space? 19

18. How does gravity work? 20

19. Where else can we see gravity at work? 21

20. Why does any of this matter to me? 22

Glossary 23

Index and Web Sites 24

The Forces That Move the World

Have you ever watched a raindrop slide down a window? How could you tell that it was moving? The way people most often sense motion is by seeing that an object's position has changed.

All motion is caused by some kind of force. For example, if you hit a baseball, it flies through the air. You use force every time you do something. Walking takes force. Opening a jar, hearing a sound, and coloring a picture all take force. In nature, storms have force and volcanoes have lots of force. Even a butterfly landing on a flower has force.

If you want to swing on a tire swing, you need force. You can get a push from a friend, as this boy is. This push will send you spinning through the air.

You use force whenever you push, pull, or lift something. Any object that gives some of its **energy** to another object is using force.

Any time you make something move, you are using force. For example, throwing a baseball, as this boy is doing, takes force.

Using your hands to move something is not the only way to use force. You also use force when you blow out the candles on a birthday cake, as this girl is doing.

You can see the force of the wind when you fly a kite. You can often feel the wind's force, too, as it pulls on the kite string.

You cannot see forces themselves. You can often see the motion that happens when a force acts on an object, though. For example, if you push a shopping cart, it moves forward. If you stomp your feet in a puddle, the water splashes everywhere. Another example is the wind. You cannot see it moving, so how do you know it has force? Think about a sailboat. The force of the wind moves the sailboat through the water.

3. Does every object take the same amount of force to move?

Heavy objects, or objects with lots of **mass**, take more force to move. A leaf blows easily in the wind, but a heavy table does not.

4. Can several forces act on an object at the same time?

Yes, they can. If the forces are equal, the object will not move. If the forces are **unbalanced**, the object will move.

Have you ever tried to lift a big pumpkin, as this girl is doing? It takes more force to lift a big, heavy pumpkin than it would to lift a smaller, lighter one.

Force that causes movement is the easiest kind to see, but it is not the only kind. When you sit on a bench, your weight pushes down. That is a force. The bench pushes back with an equal force. This is why you do not fall on the ground. If the bench's force were not equal to your force, then it would break.

These kids are playing tug-of-war. If the kids on both ends of the rope use an equal amount of force, the rope will not move. If the forces are unequal, the rope will move.

9

6. When I push something, does it always push me back?

It does. As the scientist Isaac Newton wrote, "For every action there is an equal and **opposite** reaction." This means that if you direct a force at an object, it reacts, or does something back. However, you may not feel the opposite force of the object because there are other forces acting on you.

When you jump into a pool, the force of your body dropping into the water sends water splashing up in the opposite direction.

7. Is that what happens when I let go of a balloon full of air?

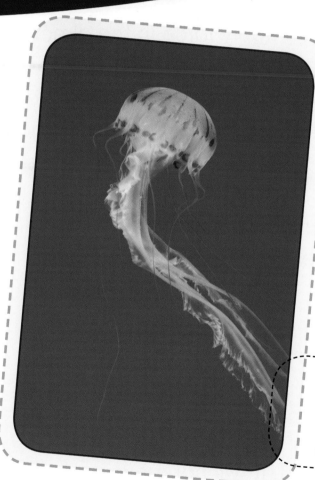

Yes, it is. When you let go of the neck of an air-filled balloon, air shoots out. The force of the air leaving causes an equal but opposite reaction in the other direction. The balloon flies through the air.

Jellyfish, such as this one, move by taking in water and shooting it out behind them. This rush of water makes the jellyfish move in the opposite direction the water does.

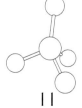

If you apply force in the direction that an object is moving, it will make the object move faster. For example, you make your bike go faster by pushing harder on your pedals. You can also use force to change the direction in which an object is moving.

To change the direction that an object is moving, you need force. If you hit a moving Ping-Pong ball across the table, you change that ball's direction.

9. Will an object move if no force acts on it?

If an object is standing still, it will not move unless some force acts on it. However, if an object is already moving, it will keep moving unless a force stops it.

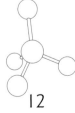

How fast something moves is its speed. In outer space, a moving object would keep moving at the same speed forever. On Earth, many forces act on objects in motion. These forces will not let a ball roll forever.

On Earth, a kicked soccer ball will roll for a while, but then it will come to a stop. The harder you kick the ball, though, the longer it will keep moving.

11. What kind of forces stop motion?

One of the forces that stops motion is **friction**. Friction happens when one object rubs against another. It causes the object to slow down over time.

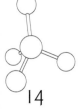

Some objects make more friction than others. Ice does not make much friction. This makes it possible to ice-skate, as these young hockey players are doing. It also makes it easy to slip on ice.

If you roll a block on the ground, it stops after a few tumbles. If you roll a ball, it moves a lot longer than the block. Soon even the ball will stop, though. The ball is smooth and round, so it has less friction acting against it than a block. Things that have flat sides or **rough** outsides are not as easy to put into motion. It takes more force to move them.

These boys are sledding down a hill. The smooth, rounded shape of their sled makes for less friction. This helps them move fast.

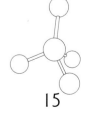

13. What force makes two magnets move toward each other?

A force called **magnetism** pulls magnets toward each other. Magnetism is what makes some things stick to your refrigerator. Magnets have two sides, called poles. One pole has a negative **electric charge**. The other pole has a positive charge.

14. Why do magnets sometimes push away from each other?

Magnetic poles with the same charge push away from each other. Poles with different electric charges are pulled toward each other.

Magnets also pull many objects that are made out of metal to them. This boy has picked up a bunch of paper clips with a magnet.

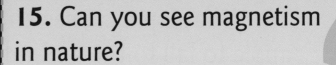

15. Can you see magnetism in nature?

This girl is using a compass. A compass has a needle that always points to Earth's magnetic north pole. Knowing which direction is north keeps people from getting lost.

Yes, magnetism is common in the natural world. As many planets do, Earth has magnetic poles. Earth's magnetism is useful. People make tools called **compasses** that use Earth's natural magnetism to tell us in what direction we are heading.

These colorful bands in the sky are the northern lights. They are also known as the aurora borealis. They are caused by Earth's magnetism.

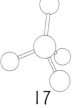

16. What force causes an apple to fall to the ground?

Have you ever seen apples or leaves falling from a tree? Have you wondered what makes those things fall? They fall because of a force called **gravity**. Gravity pulls everything on Earth toward the planet's center. Thanks to gravity, we do not all float off into space!

Though getting a push or pumping your legs can send you high into the air on a swing, gravity will soon pull you back down.

17. Why can't I kick a ball into outer space?

The ball would be pulled back to Earth by gravity. Instead of flying off into space in a straight line, it would go up and then begin to fall back down toward the ground. If your ball had **rocket boosters** on it, you might have better luck. The boosters could give it enough power to break free from Earth's gravity and head into space.

This girl is juggling. The fact that gravity causes a ball thrown into the air to fall back to Earth is what makes juggling possible.

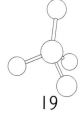

19

18. How does gravity work?

Gravity is a natural force. It pulls any two objects with mass together. Big objects have a much stronger gravitational pull than smaller ones do. Most objects are too small for us to sense gravity pulling them toward each other. However, the gravitational pull of huge objects, such as planets, is strong enough to pull small objects, such as people, toward them.

No matter how high you jump, gravity will always pull you back to Earth.

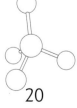

19. Where else can we see gravity at work?

Gravity is the reason why stars, moons, and planets move the ways they do. Gravity keeps Earth circling the Sun. It also holds the Moon in its **orbit**. The Moon's gravity causes tides on Earth.

Gravity is such a strong force that it holds together galaxies, such as the one in this picture. Galaxies are huge groups of stars and planets. Earth is in the Milky Way galaxy.

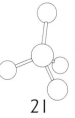

20. Why does any of this matter to me?

You and everything in the world around you deal with many different forces each day. From gravity to hitting a baseball, we deal with forces all the time.

The world is also always in motion. Even the smallest **particles**, called atoms, are always moving around. Many useful inventions were made possible through an understanding of forces and motion. There is a lot more to learn. Just keep asking questions!

While gravity pulls all objects back to Earth, a force called lift keeps hang gliders, like this one, in the air. Lift is caused by the movement of air over the glider's curved wing.

Glossary

compasses (KUM-pus-ez) Tools made up of a freely turning magnetic needle that tells which direction is north.

electric charge (ih-LEK-trik CHAHRJ) Something some matter has that can produce power.

energy (EH-ner-jee) The power to work or to act.

friction (FRIK-shin) The rubbing of one thing against another.

gravity (GRA-vih-tee) The force that causes objects to move toward each other. The bigger an object is, the more gravity it has.

magnetism (MAG-nuh-tih-zum) The force that pulls certain objects toward a magnet.

mass (MAS) The amount of matter in something.

opposite (AH-puh-zut) Totally and exactly different.

orbit (OR-bit) A circular path.

particles (PAR-tih-kulz) Small pieces of matter.

rocket boosters (RAH-kit BOO-sterz) Rockets on a bigger rocket or a spacecraft that add power.

rough (RUF) Not smooth.

unbalanced (un-BA-luntst) Not balanced, or unequal.

Index

A
air, 4, 11

B
baseball, 4, 22

E
electric charge, 16

F
friction, 14–15

G
gravity, 18–22

M
magnetism, 16–17
mass, 8, 20

N
Newton, Isaac, 10

O
object(s), 4, 6–8, 10,
   12, 13–14, 20
orbit, 21

P
particles, 22

people, 4, 17, 20
position, 4

R
raindrop, 4
rocket boosters, 19

S
speed, 13

W
walking, 4
water, 7
wind, 7–8

Web Sites

Due to the changing nature of Internet links, Powerkids Press has developed an online list of Web sites related to the subject of this book. This site is updated regularly. Please use this link to access the list:
www.powerkidslinks.com/quest/fm/